Douche Bag

BIRB SWEAR

Wondrous Swear Word To Color

#.or Stress Releasing

Charity Borsberry

Happy Coloring!

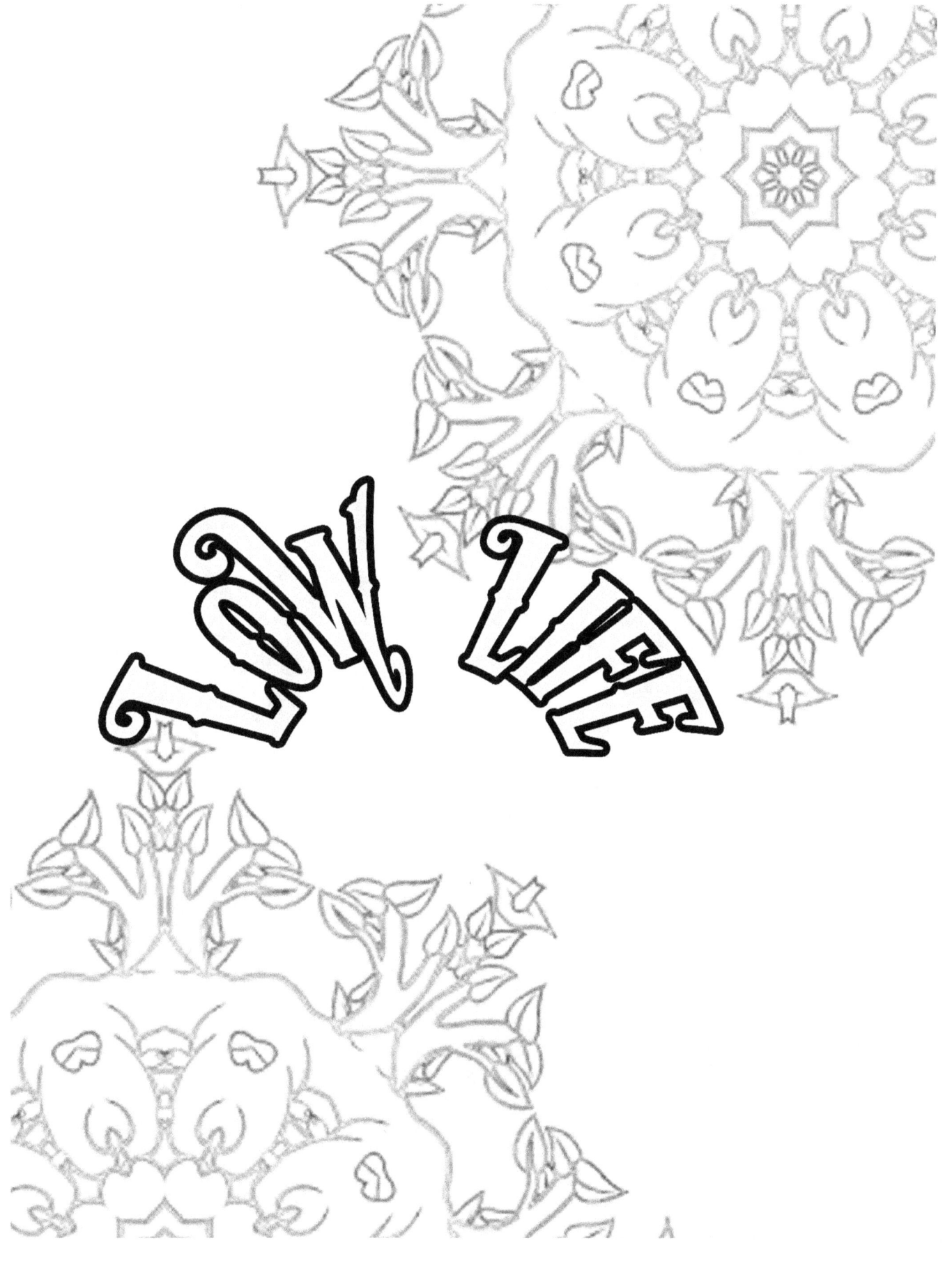

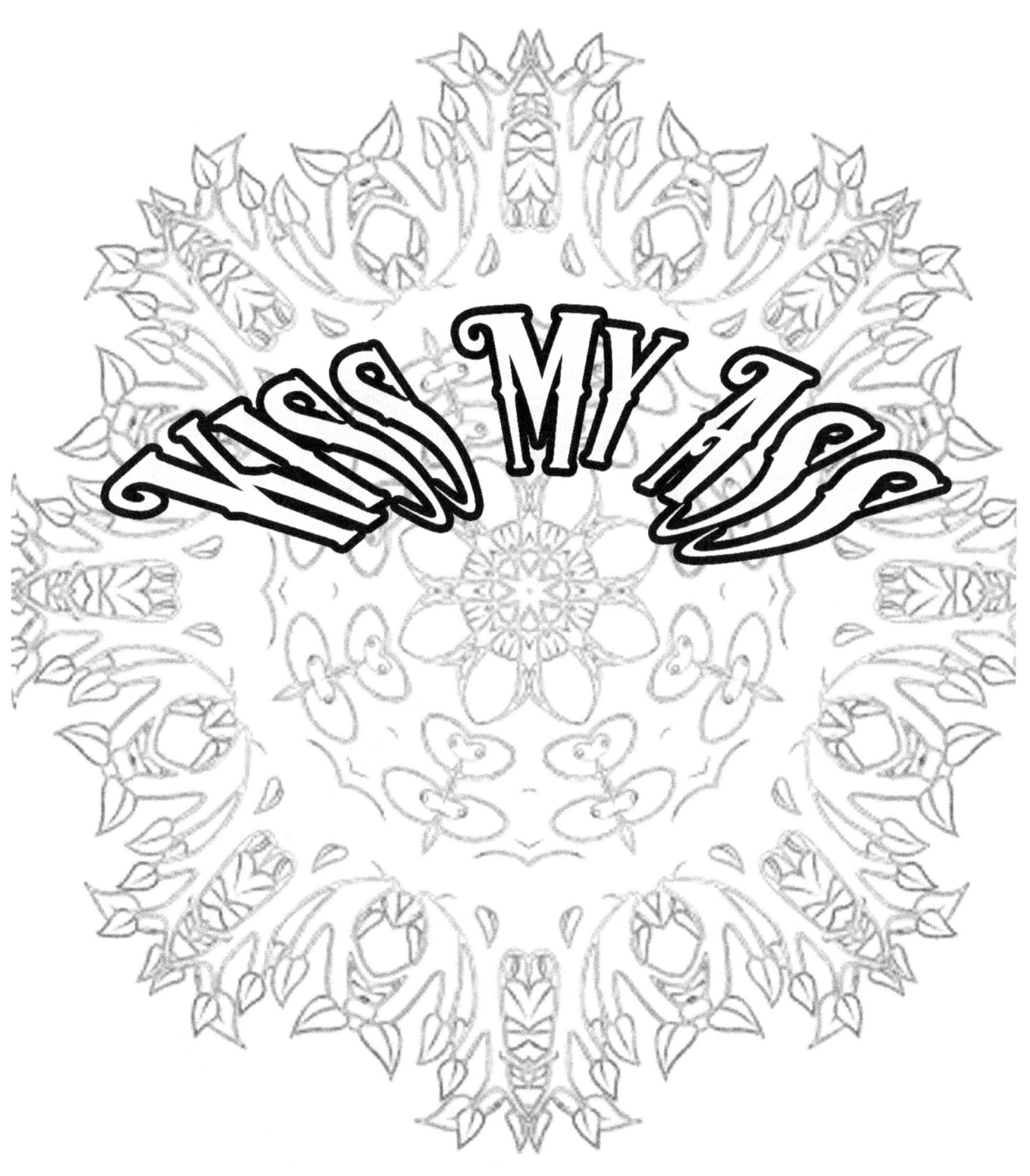

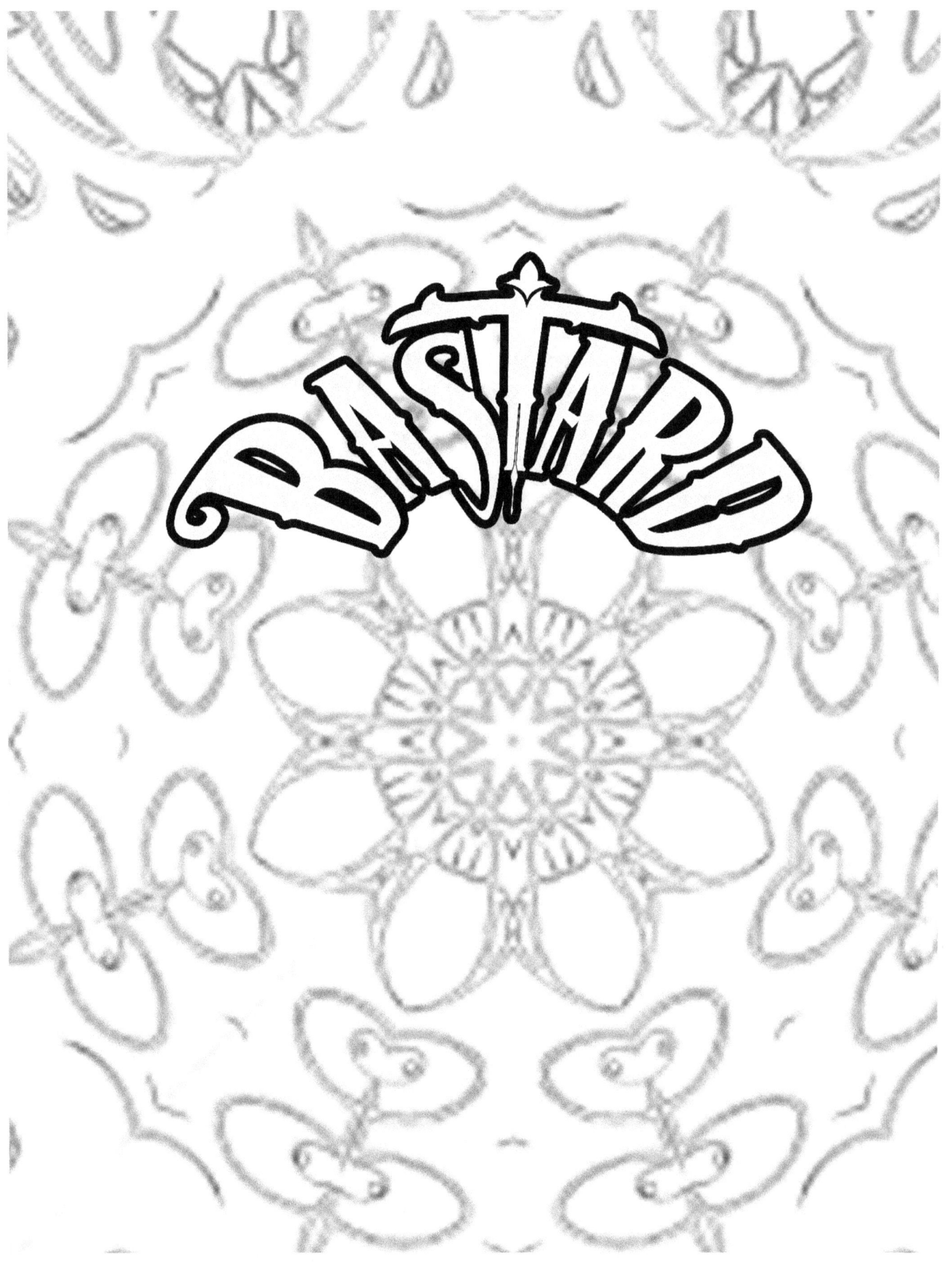

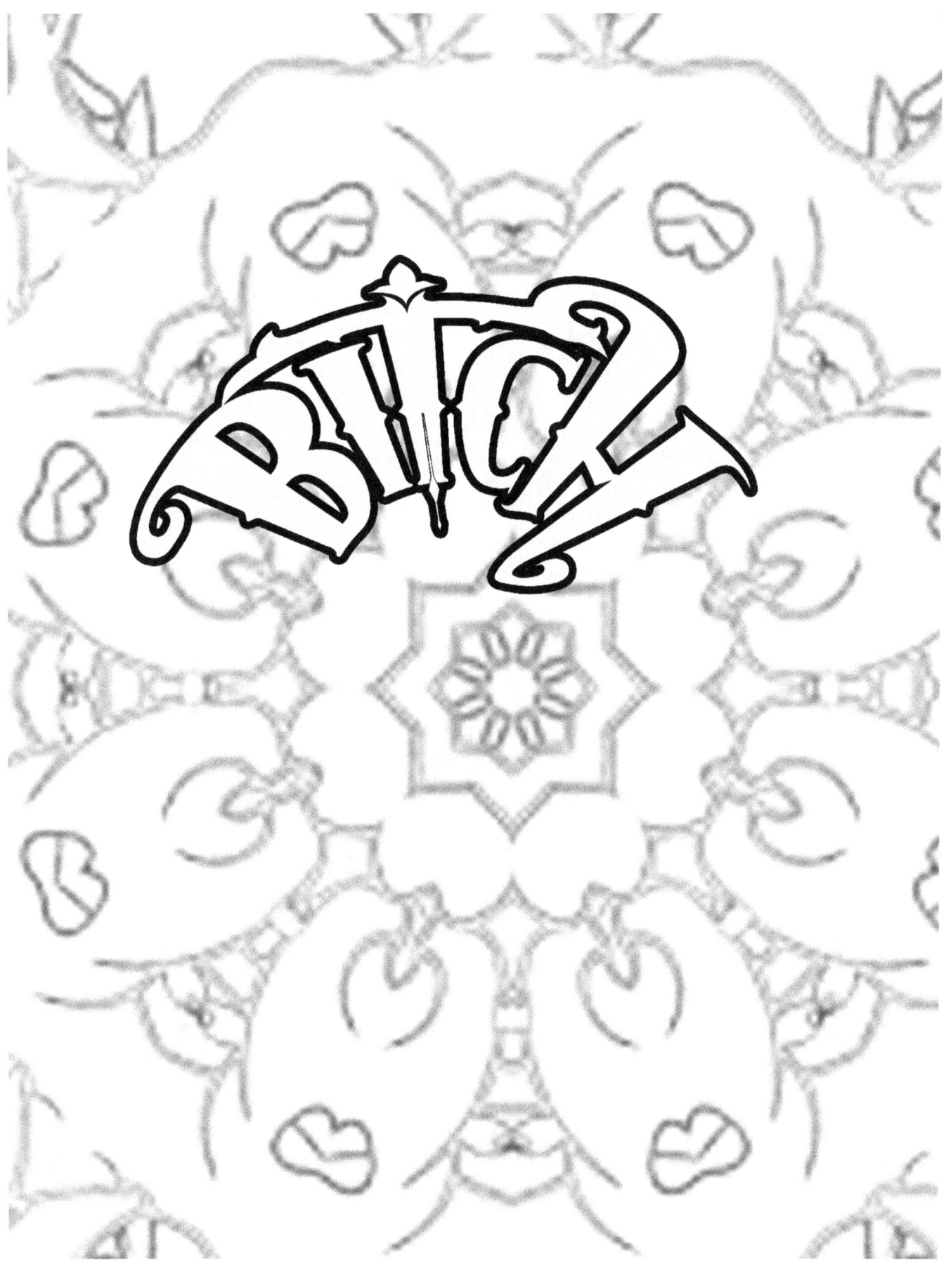

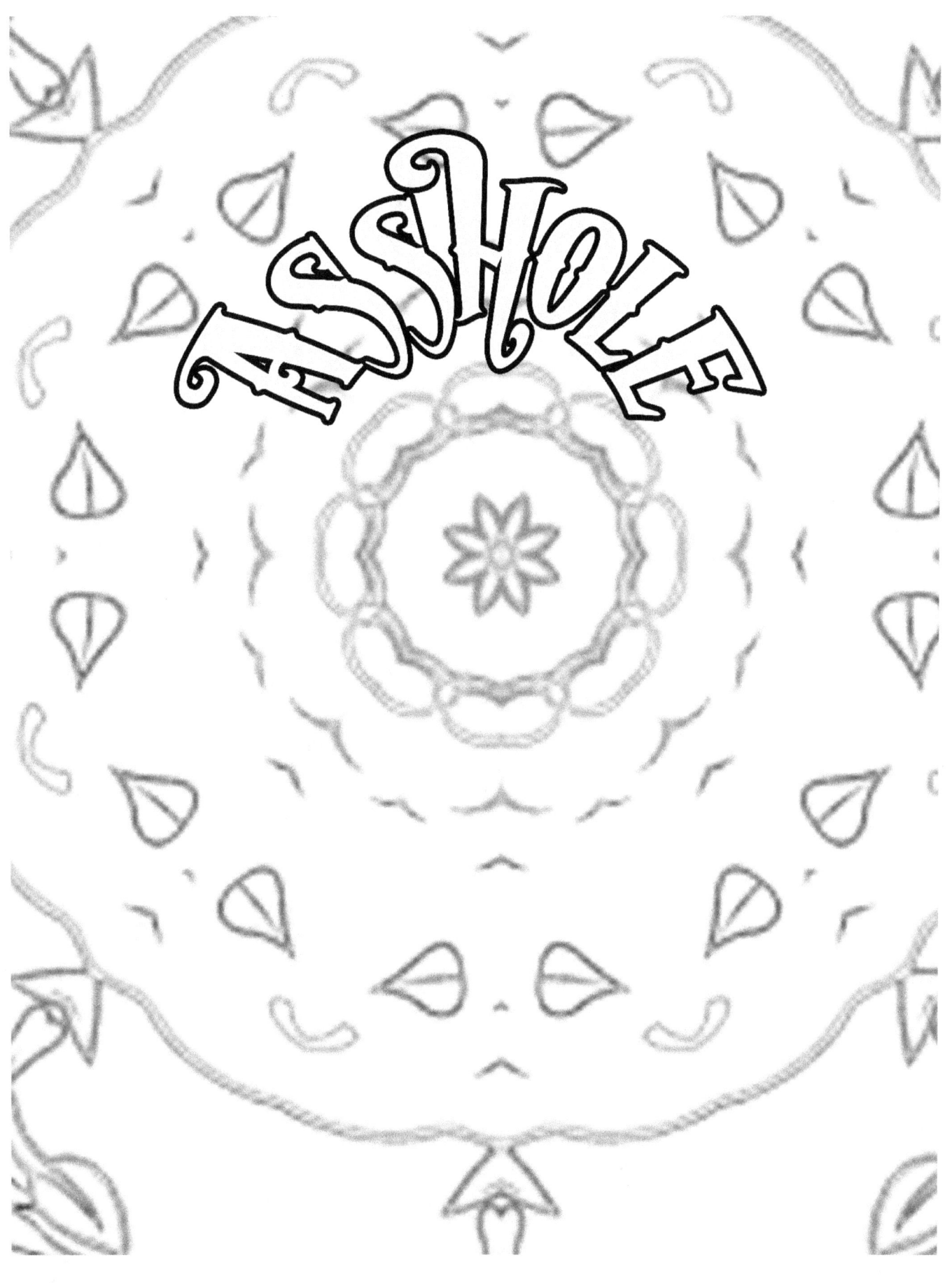

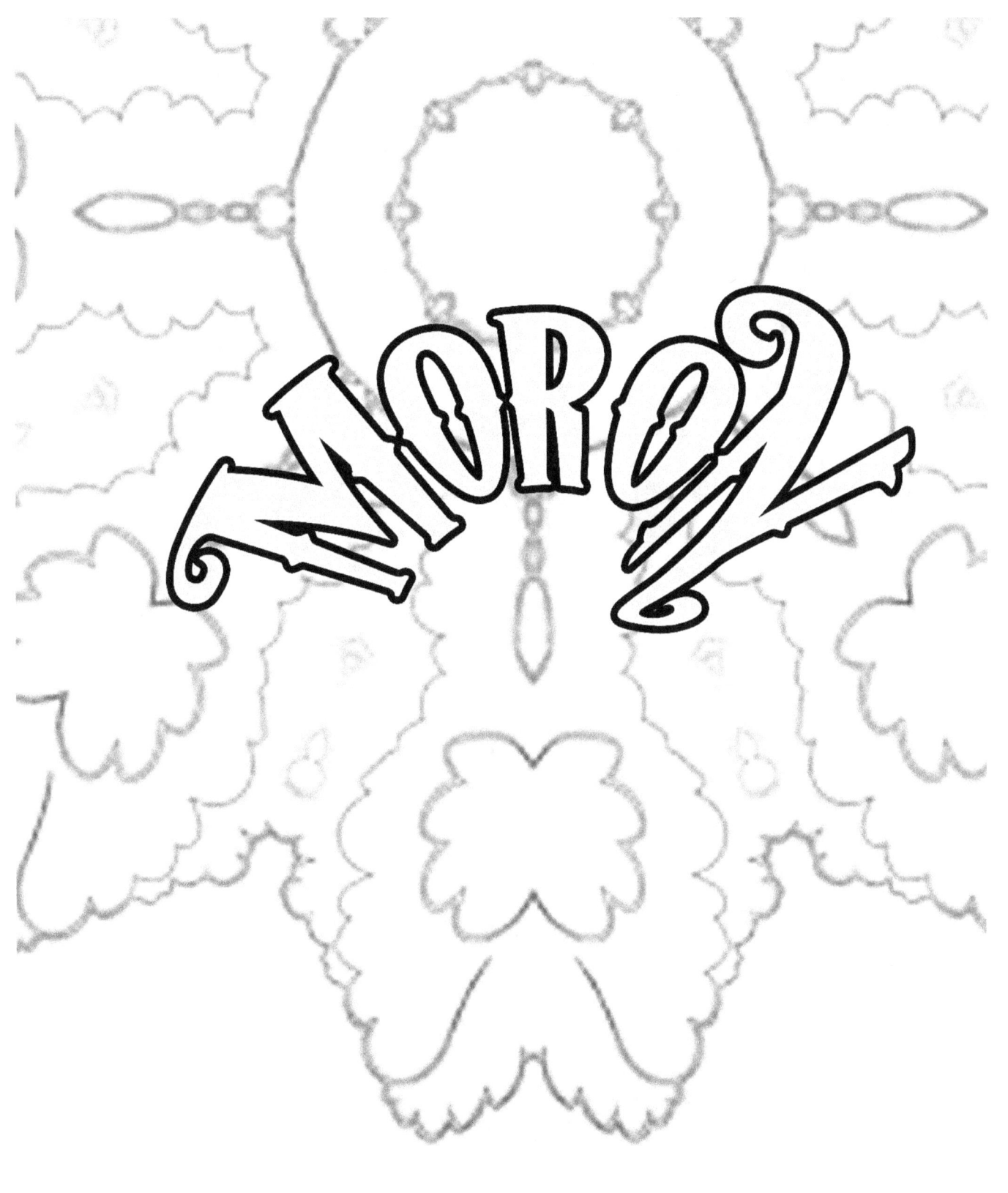

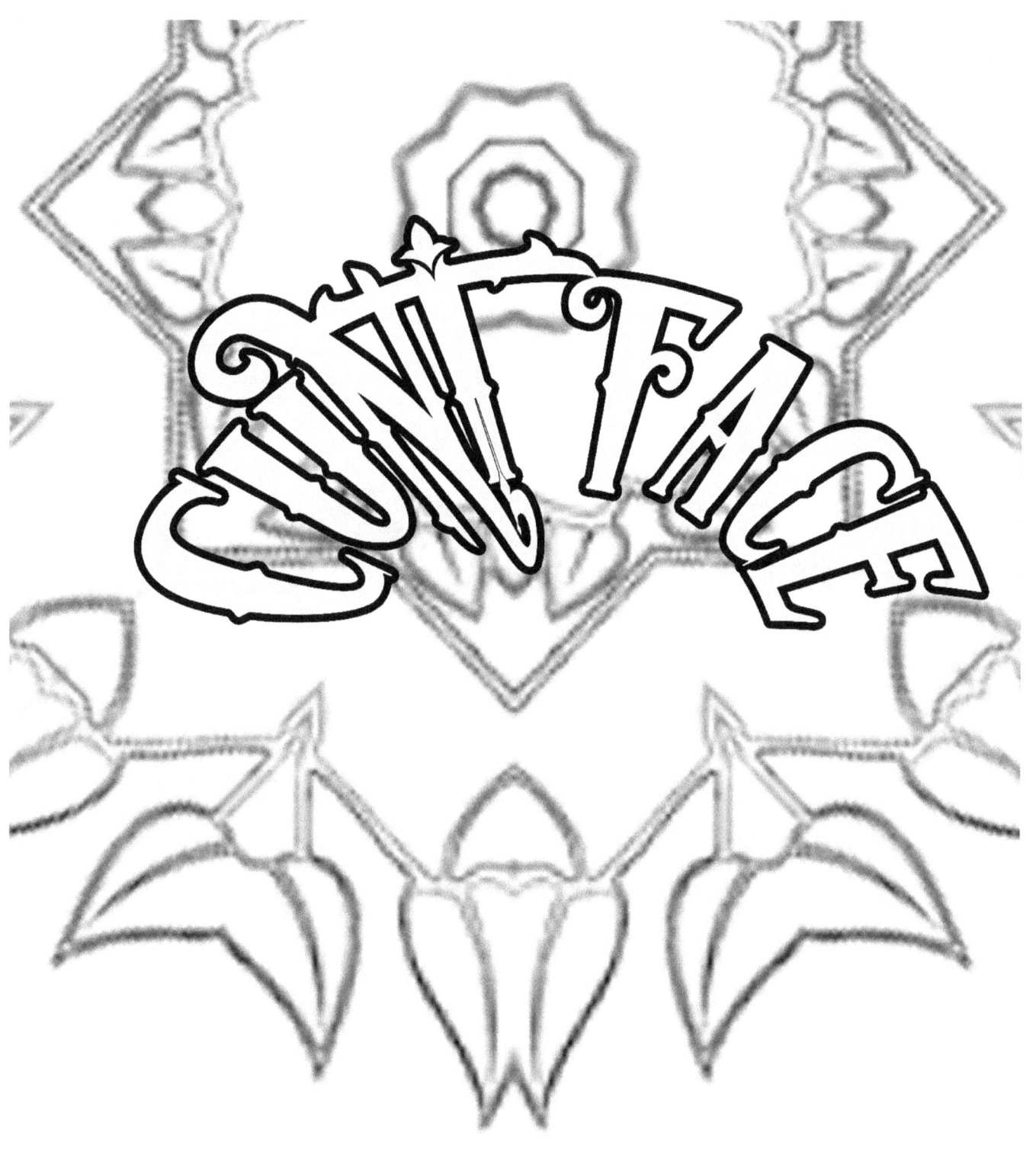

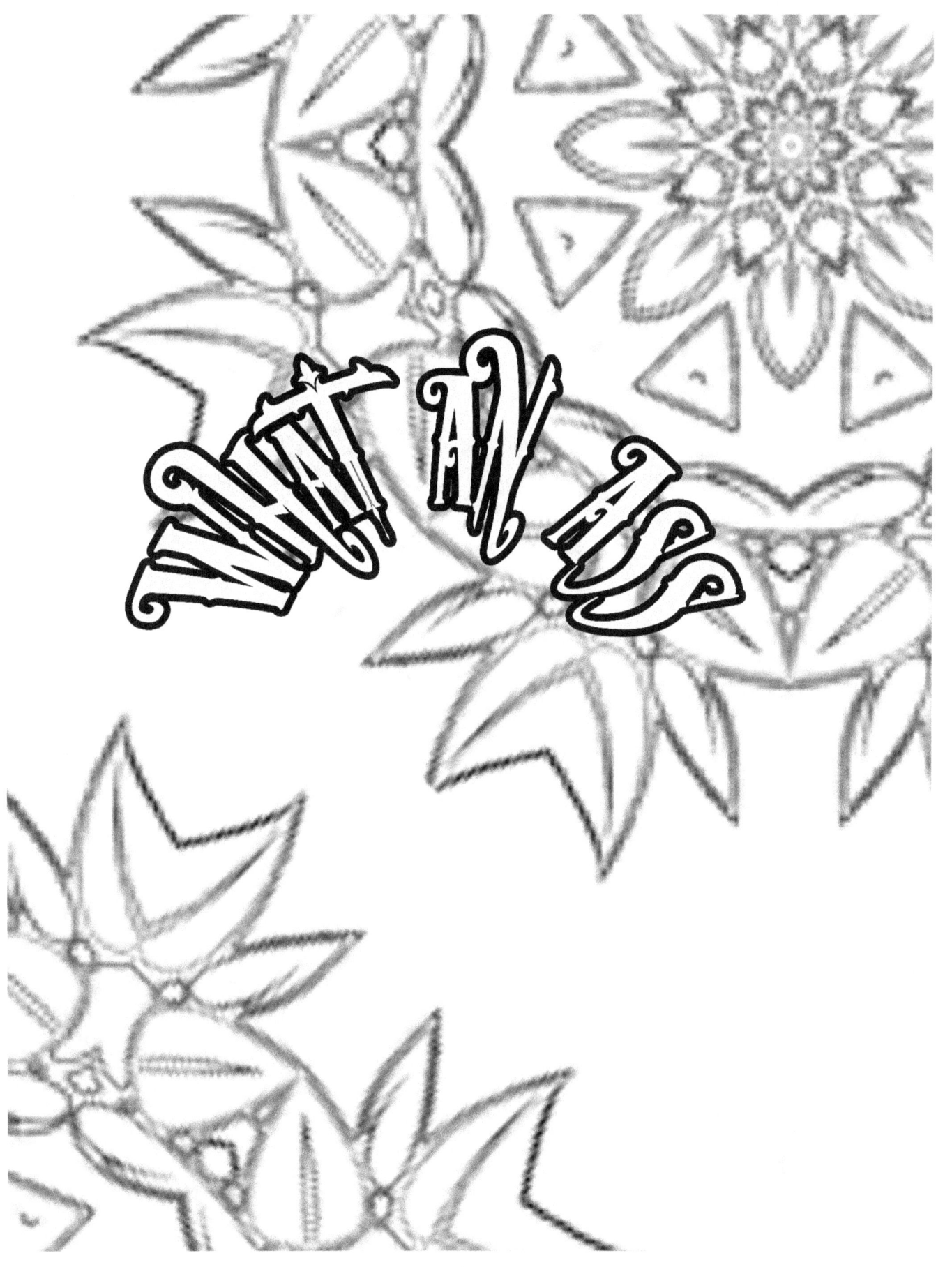

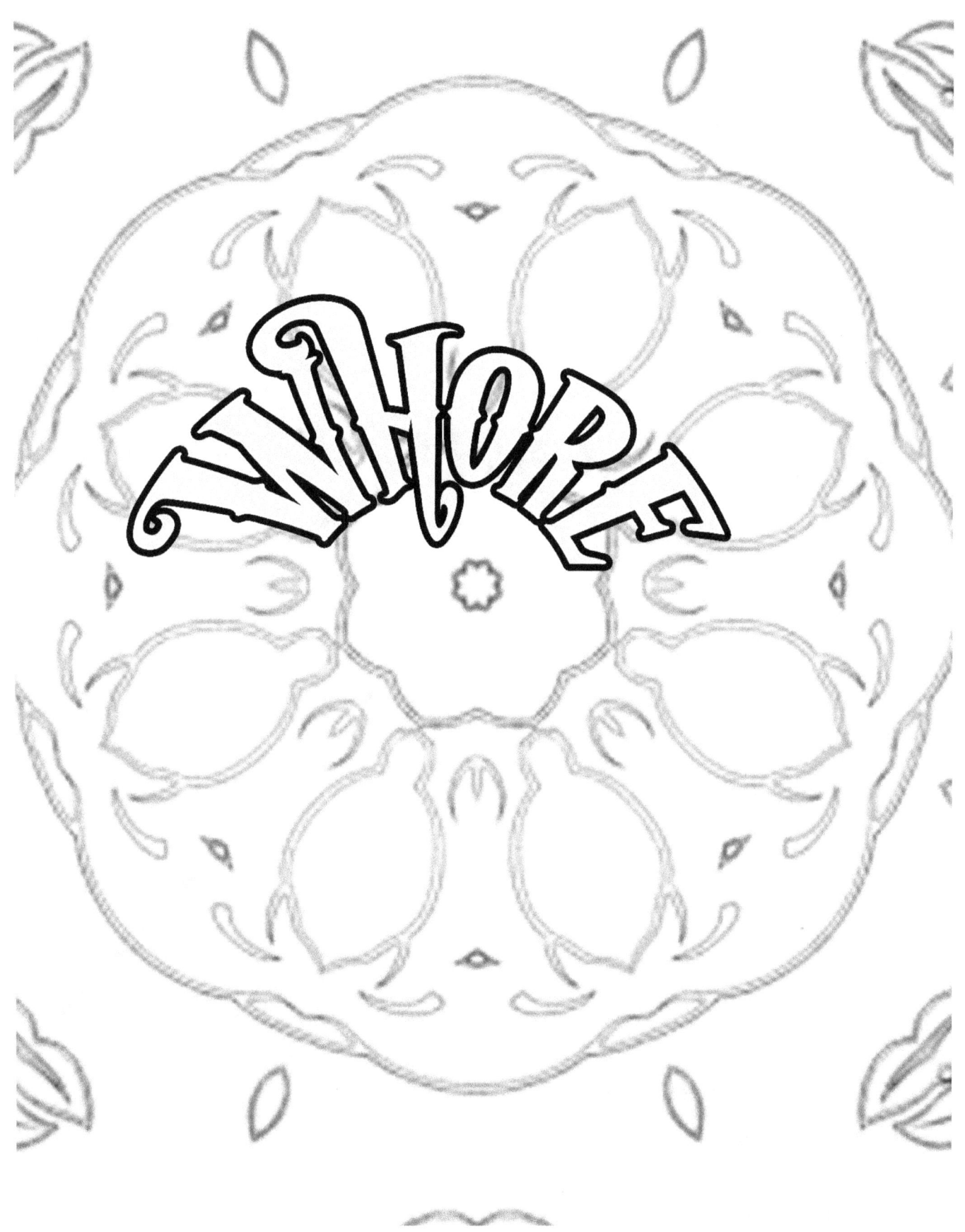

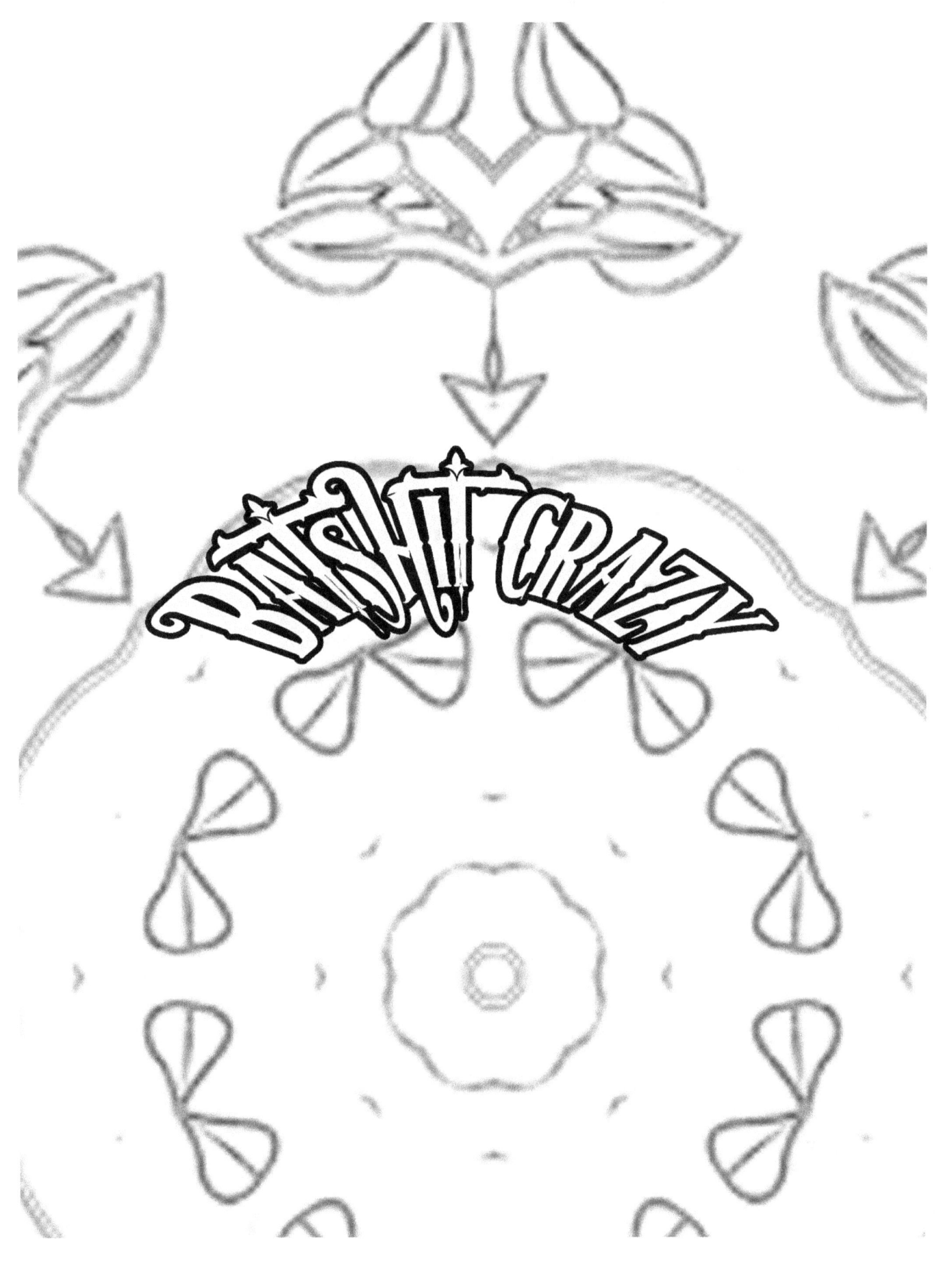

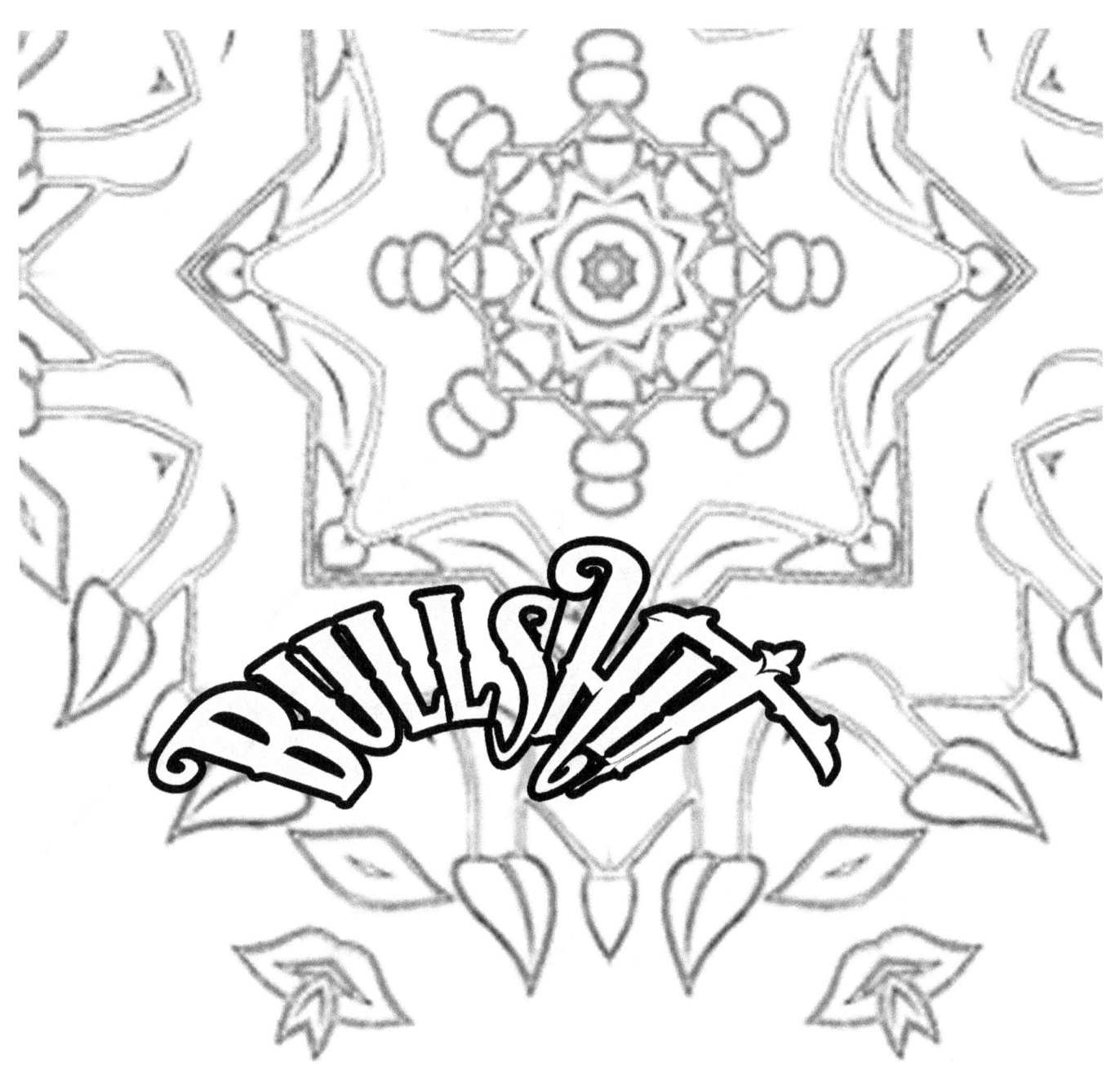

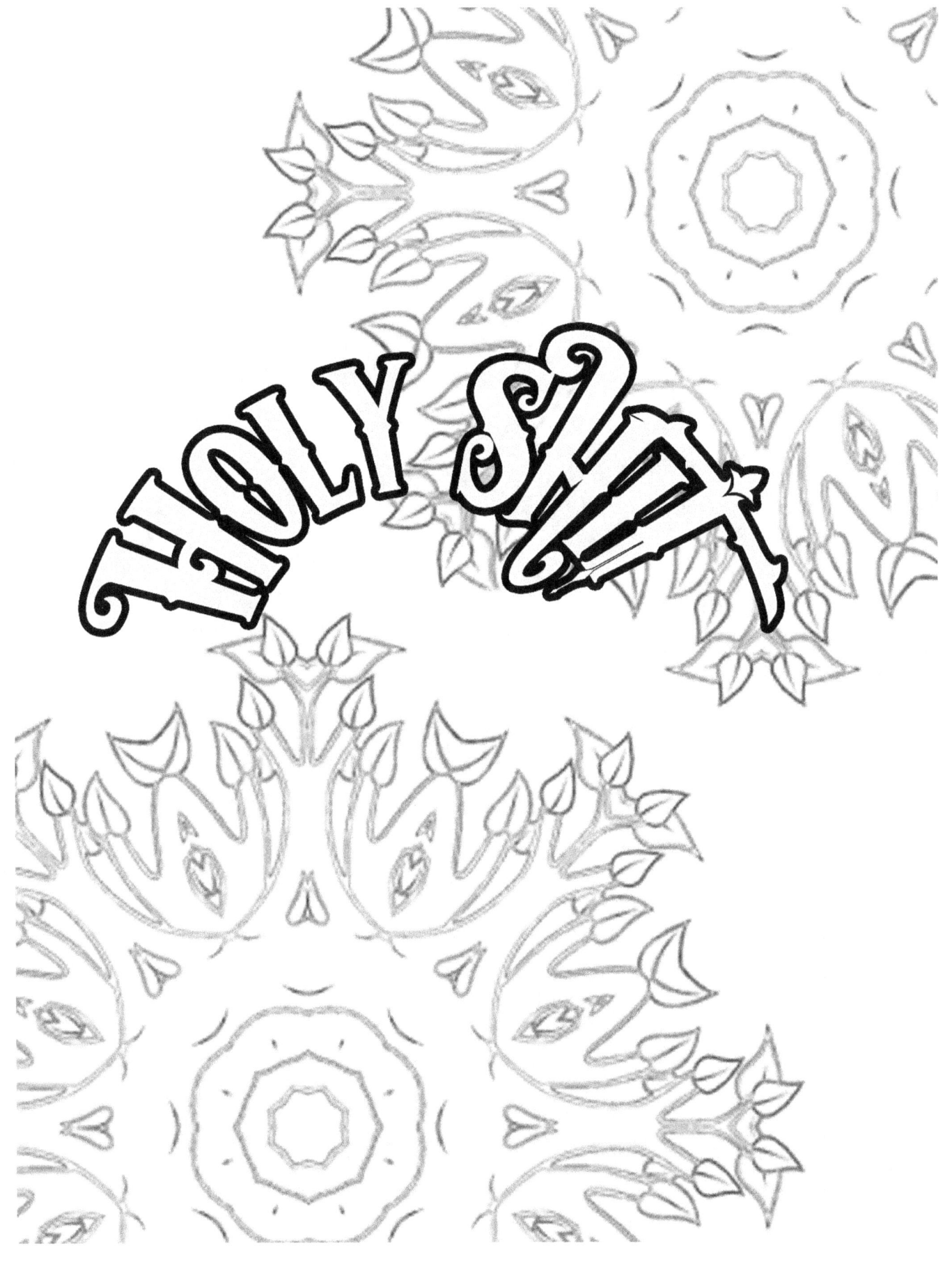

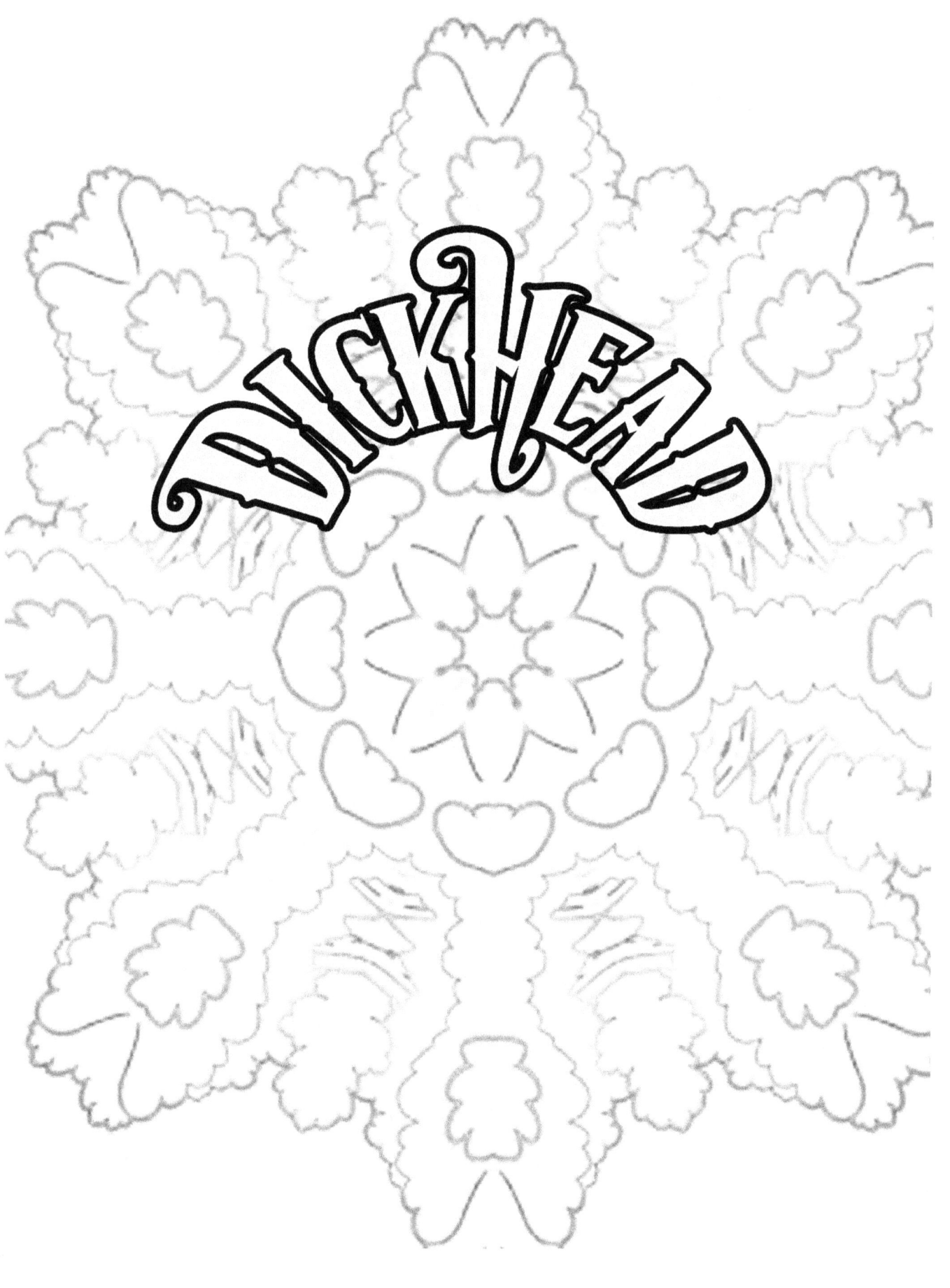

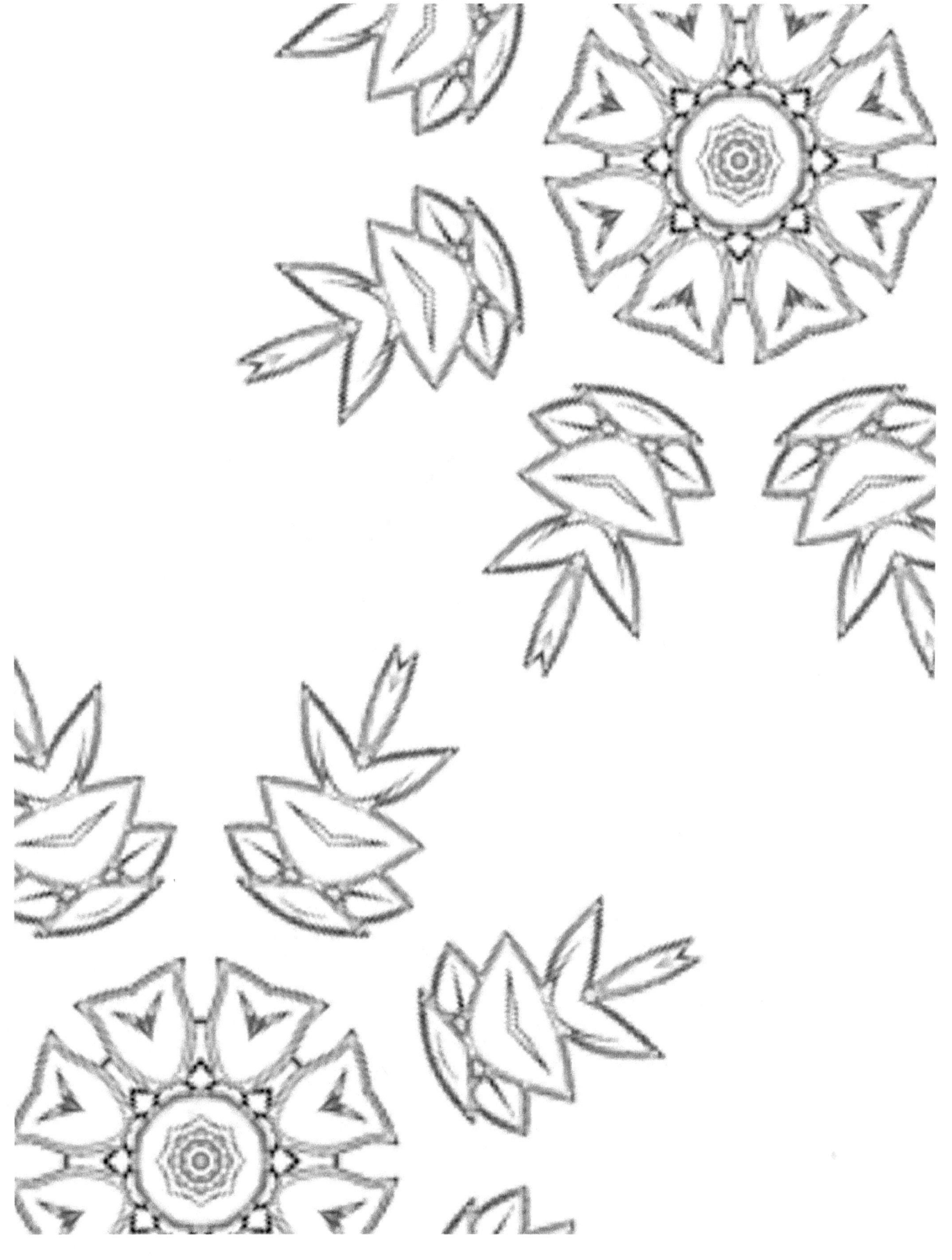

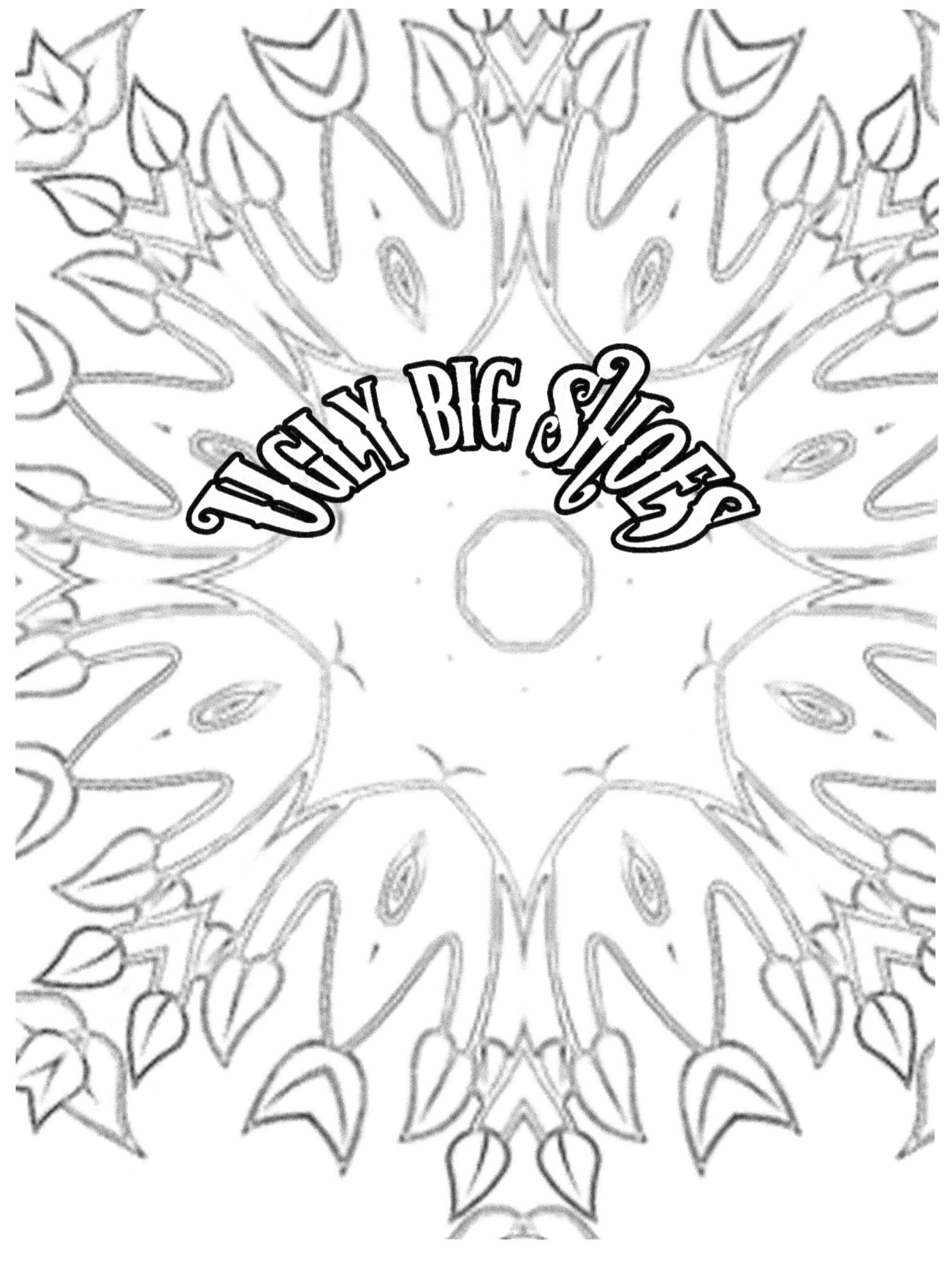

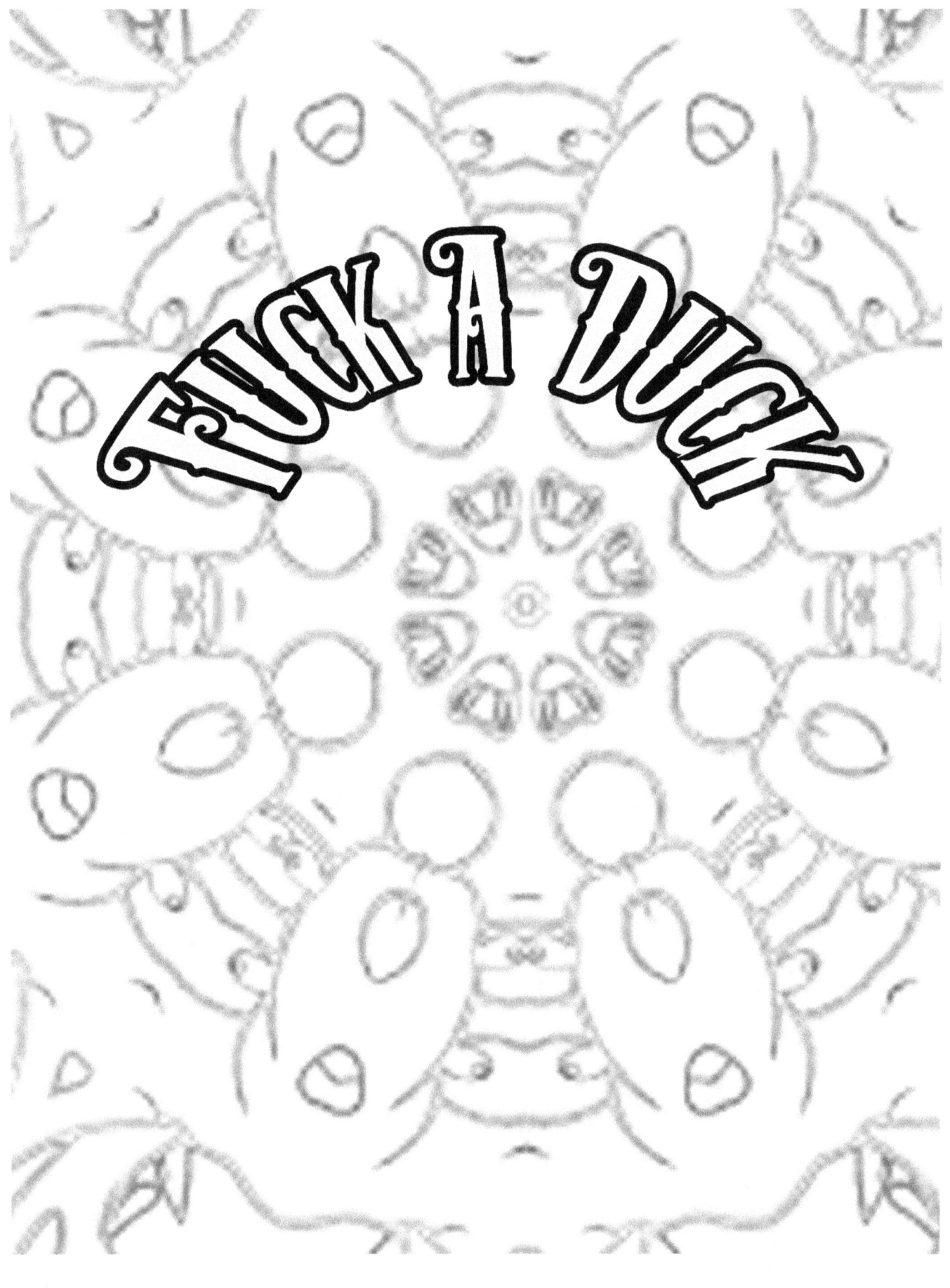

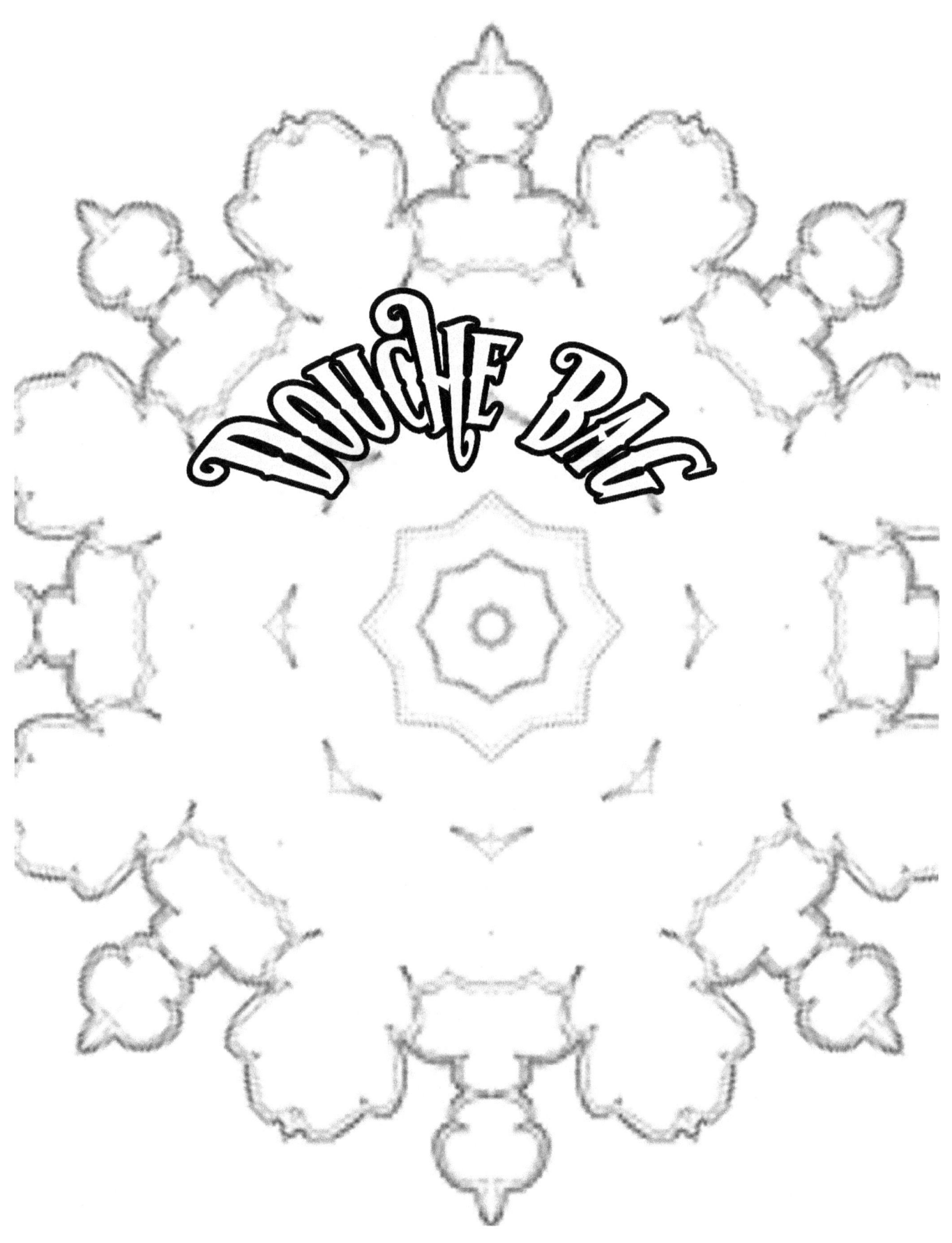

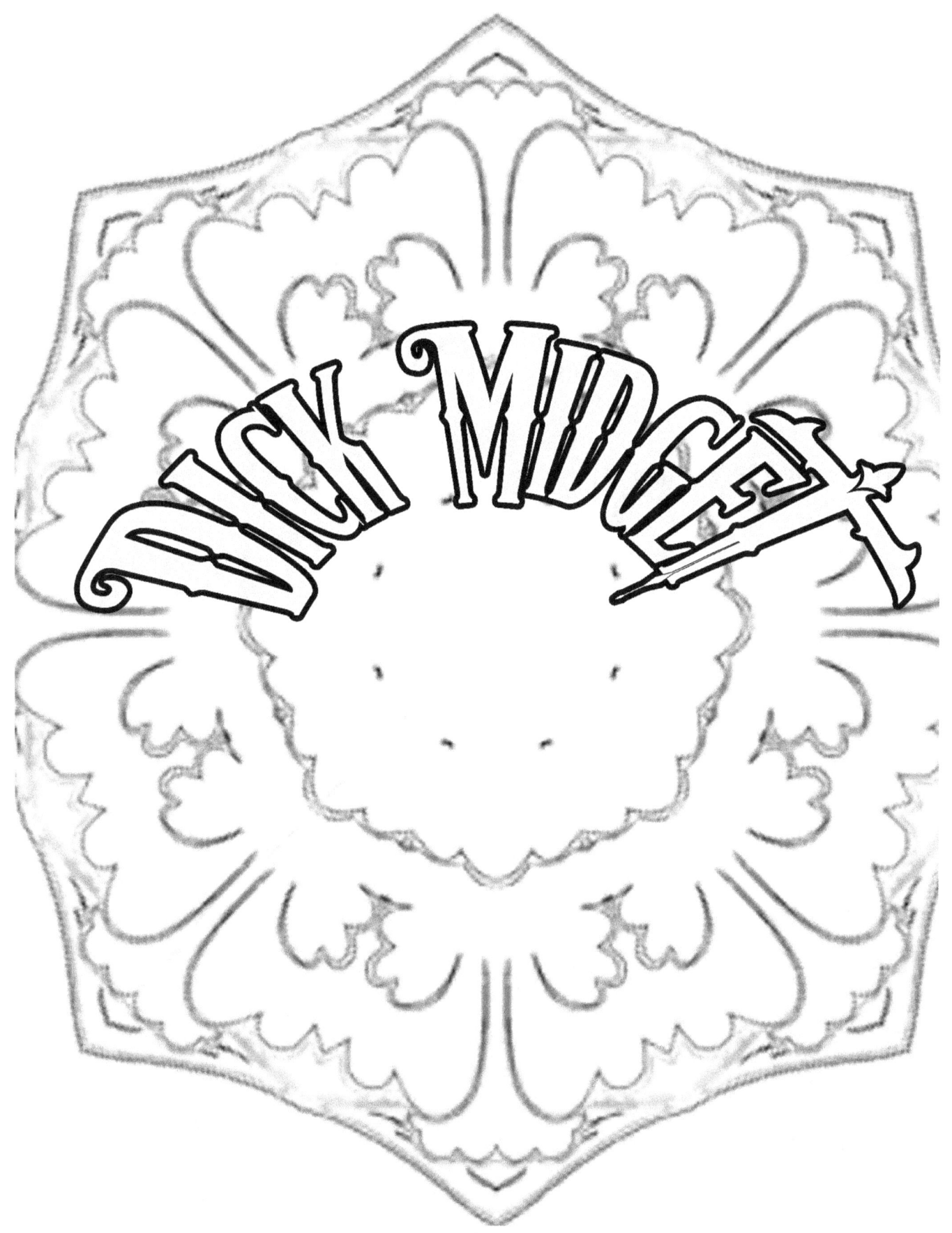

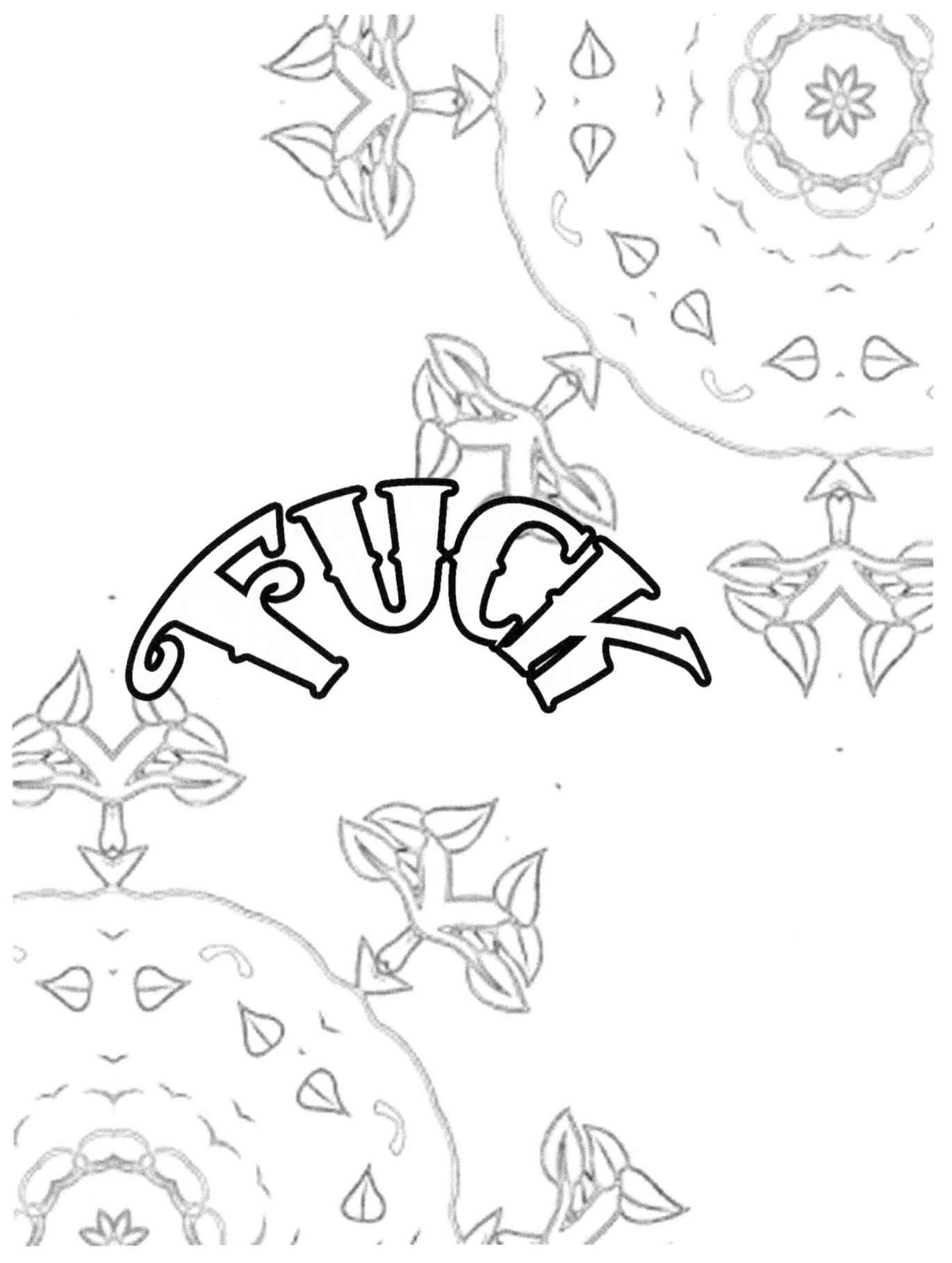

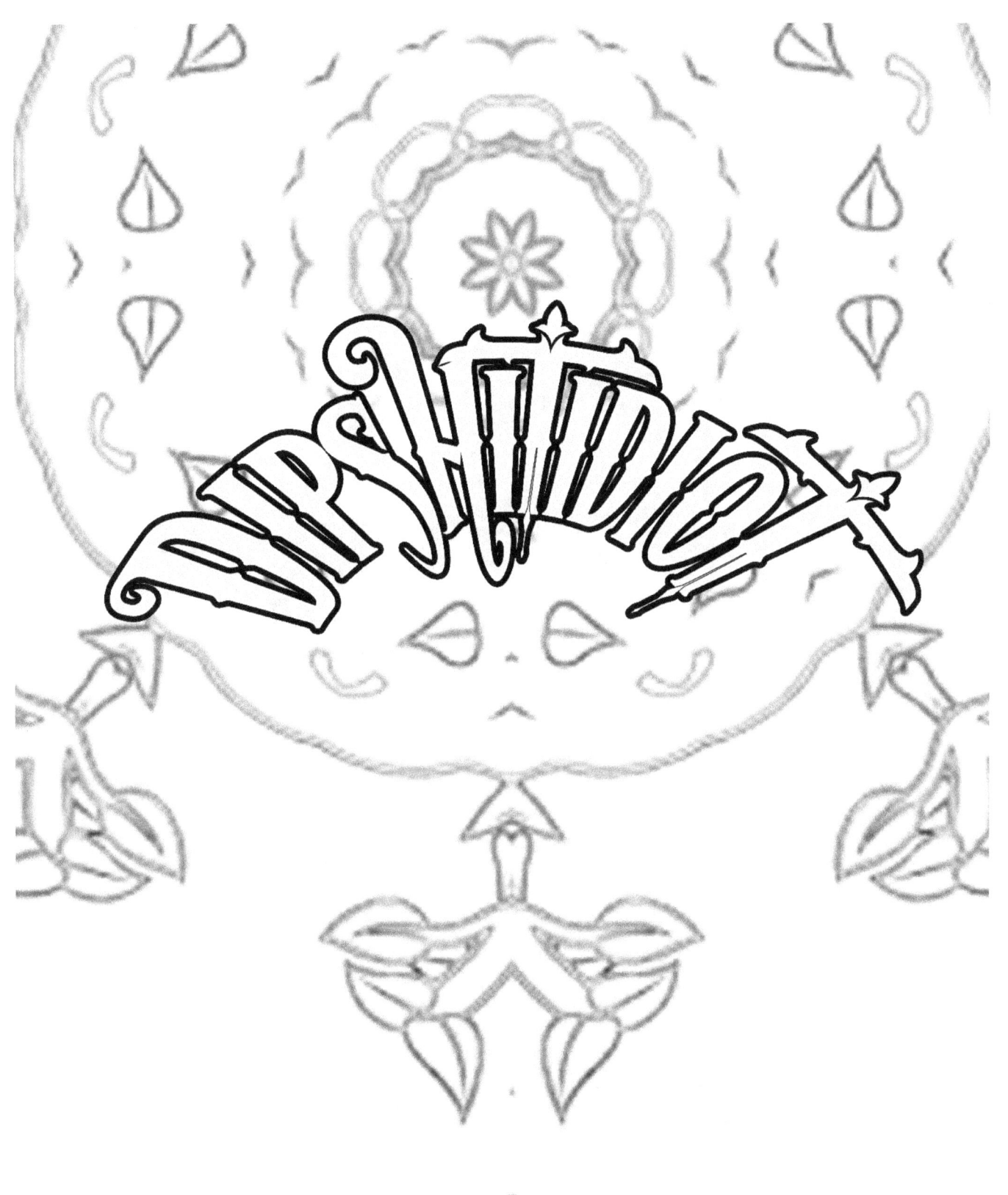

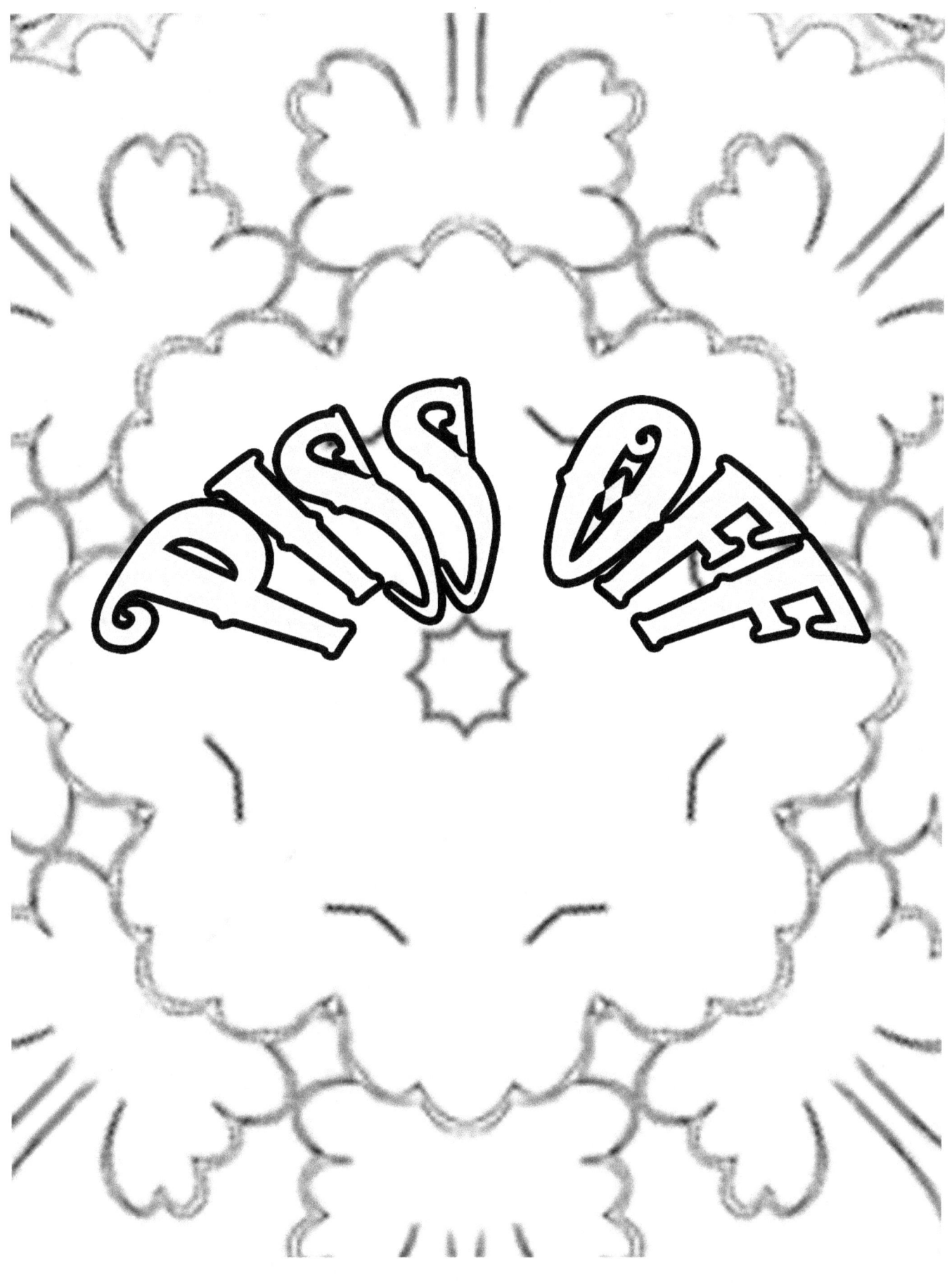

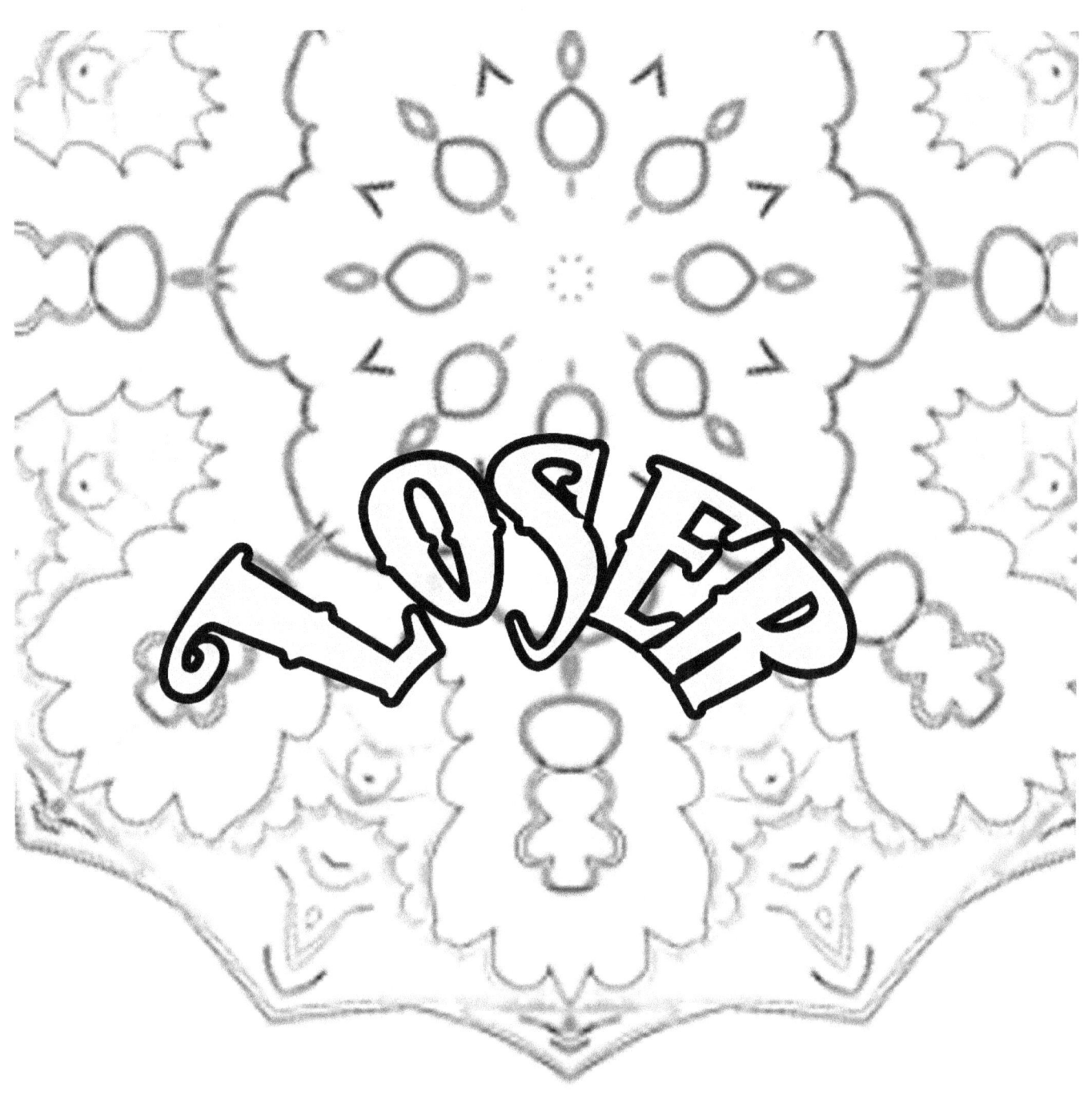

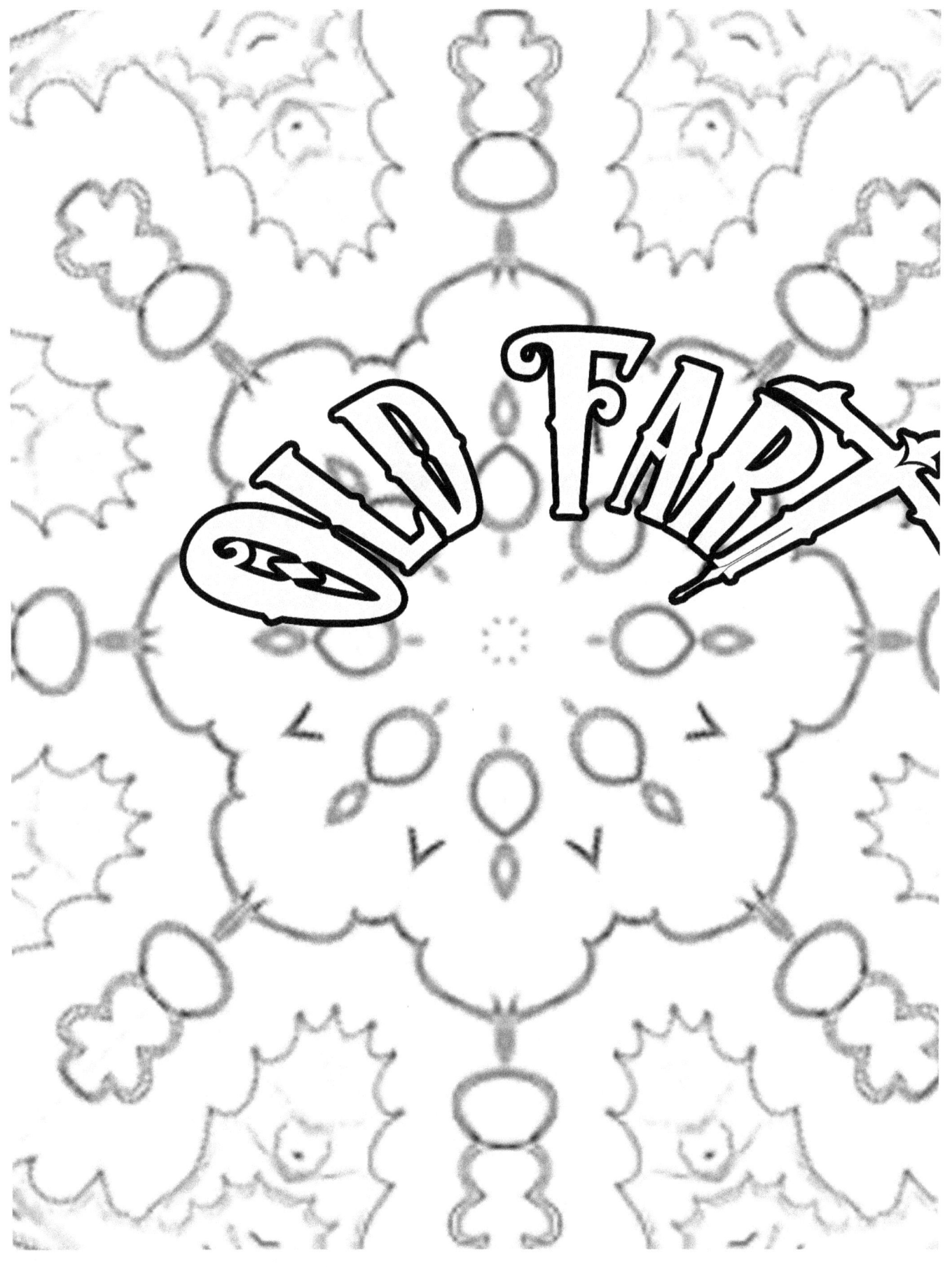

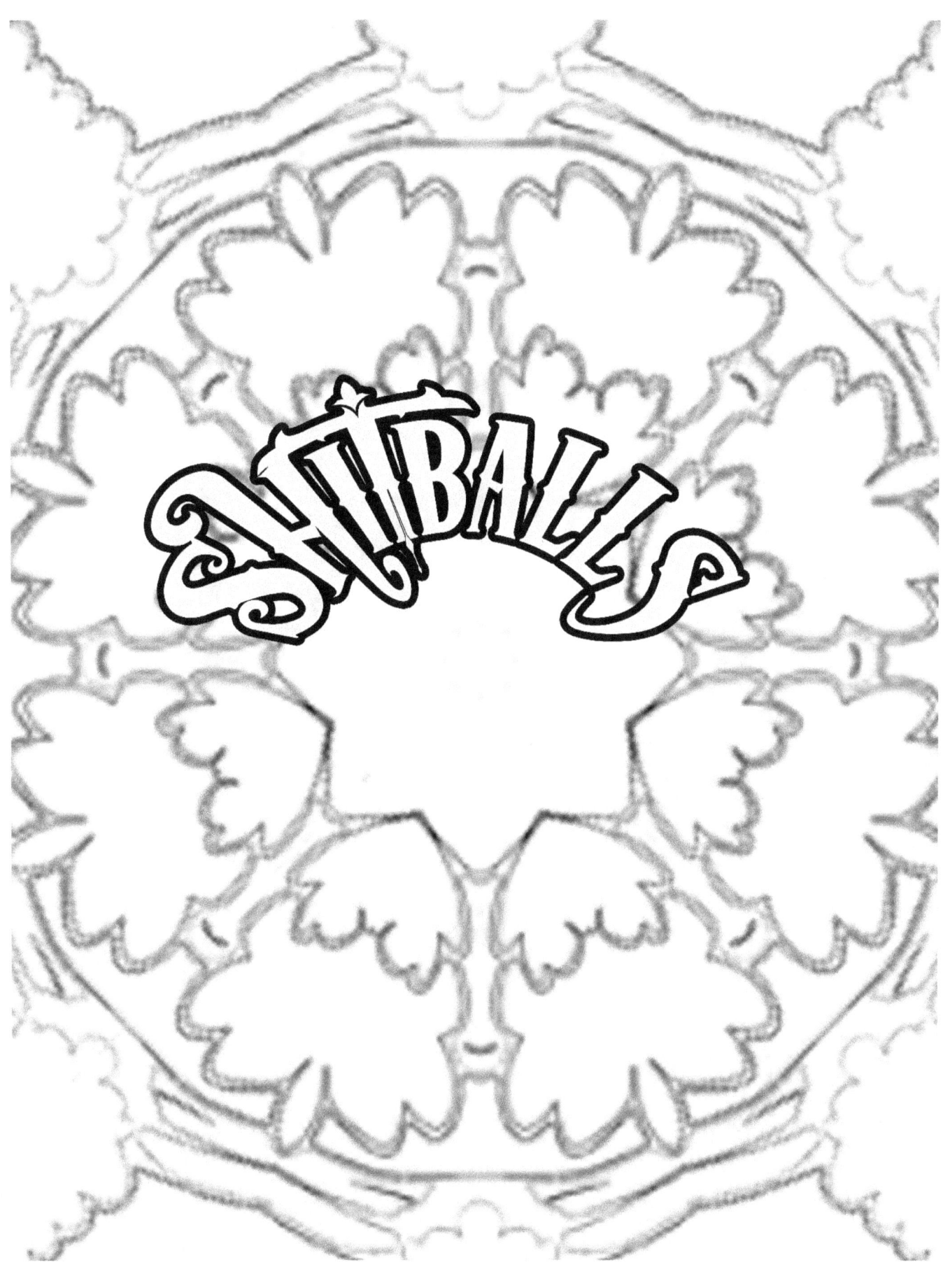

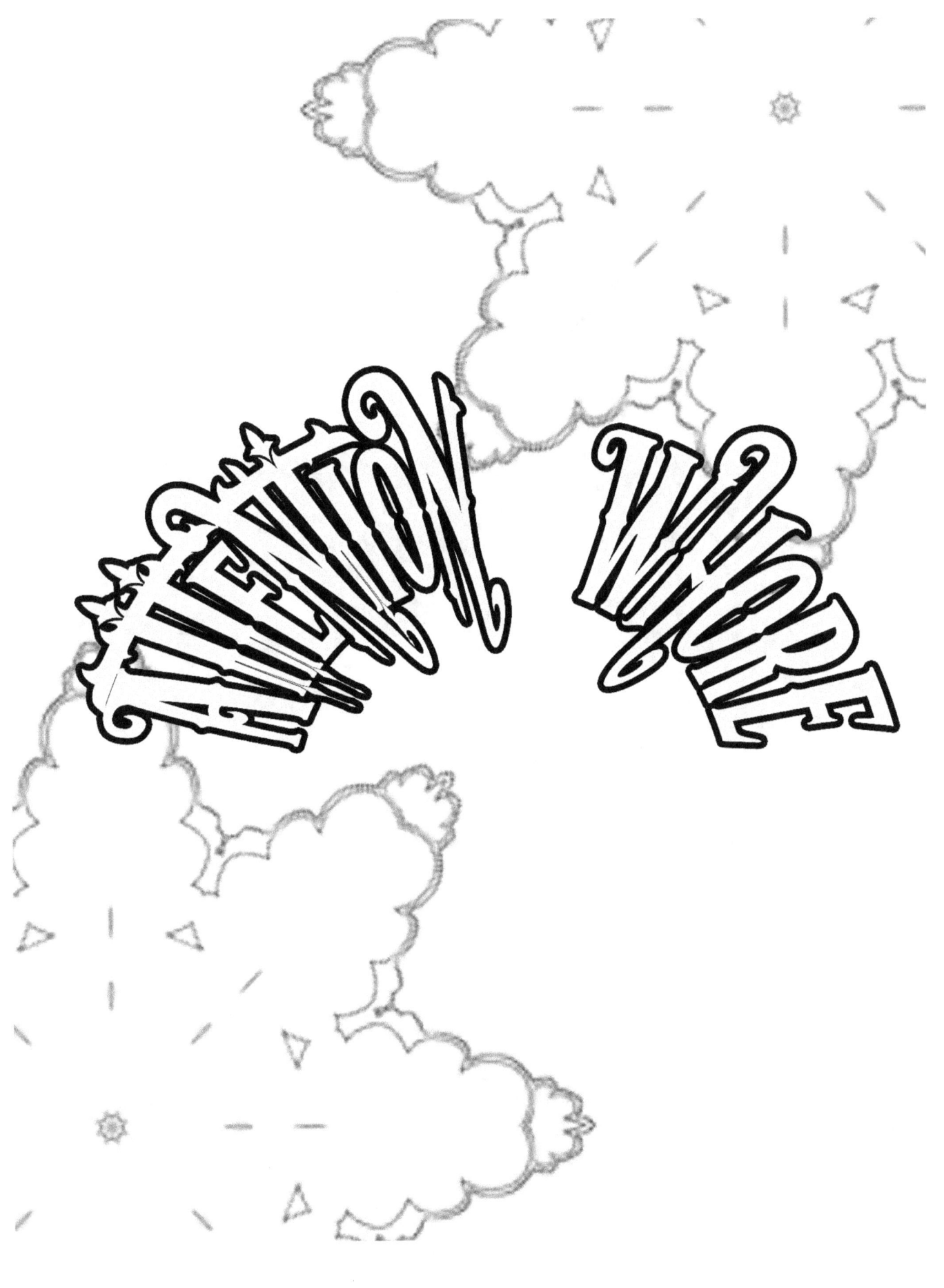

www.ingramcontent.com/pod-product-compliance
Lightning Source LLC
Chambersburg PA
CBHW081749170526
45167CB00009B/3971